BLOOMFIELD TOWNSHIP PUBLIC LIBRARY
3 1160 00557 4913

P9-CRC-716

It's Not Catching

Asthma

Angela Royston

a division of Reed Elsevier Inc.
Chicago, Illinois

Customer Service 888-454-2279

Visit our website at www.heinemannlibrary.com

Designed by Dave Oakley, Arnos Design
Artwork by Art Construction
Originated by Dot Gradations Ltd
Printed and bound in China
by South China Printing Company

08 07 06 05 04
10 9 8 7 6 5 4 3 2 1

**Library of Congress
Cataloging-in-Publication Data**
Royston, Angela.
Asthma / Angela Royston.
v. cm. -- (It's not catching)
Includes bibliographical references and index.
Contents: What is asthma? -- Who has asthma? -- What triggers an attack?-- Allergies -- Worry -- Narrow airways -- Tight chest -- Coughing -- Testing for asthma -- Inhalers -- Keeping calm -- Going to the hospital-- Preventing an attack.
ISBN 1-4034-4821-3 (hbk.)
1. Asthma--Juvenile literature. [1. Asthma.] I. Title: It's not catching, Asthma. II. Title.
RC591.R69 2004
616.2'38--dc22

2003019708

Acknowledgments
The author and publishers are grateful to the following for permission to reproduce copyright material: p. 4 Powerstock/Bluestone; pp. 5, 18, 24, 25, 28, 29 Phillip James Photography; p. 6 Getty Images/Patrisha Thomson; p. 7 Alamy/Mark Andersen; p. 8 Getty Images/Yellow Dog Productions; p. 9 Trevor Clifford; p. 10 SPL/Andy Hammond; p. 11 Dave Bradford; p. 12 SPL/Labat Jerrican; p. 13 Getty Images/Pauline Cutler; p. 16 SPL/BSIP DUCLOUX; p. 17 SPL/BSIP/Laurent/ Bouhier; p. 19 Last Resort Photo Library/Jo Makin; p. 20 Getty Images/Gary Buss; p. 21 SPL/Damien Lovegrove; p. 22 Gareth Boden; p. 23 SPL/GUSTO; p. 26 John Birdsall Picture Library; p. 27 SPL/Mauro Fermariello.

Cover photograph reproduced with permission of Angela Hampton.

The publishers would like to thank David Wright for his assistance in the preparation of this book.

Every effort has been made to contact copyright holders of any material reproduced in this book. Any omissions will be rectified in subsequent printings if notice is given to the publisher.

Contents

Some words are shown in bold, **like this.** You can find out what they mean by looking in the glossary.

What Is Asthma?

Many people who have **asthma** breathe normally most of the time. You cannot tell they have asthma. But they may cough often and get out of breath easily.

Sometimes coughing can bring on an asthma attack. When this happens, the person has a hard time breathing. Their breathing may make a wheezing or whistling sound.

Who Has Asthma?

Many people have **asthma.** You cannot catch asthma from someone else. Asthma is the way some people **react** to things that **irritate** their **lungs.**

You are more likely to have asthma if your parents are **allergic** to things such as animals or dust. Children usually have fewer and fewer asthma attacks as they grow older.

What Triggers an Attack?

Many different things can cause an **asthma** attack. Running around or other **energetic** exercise can bring on an attack, especially in cold weather.

Sicknesses such as colds and flu can cause attacks, too. Even if you do not have asthma, these sicknesses make you cough and make it harder to breathe.

Allergies

Some people are **allergic** to dust or to **pollen** from flowers. This **allergy** makes them sneeze and cough. It may also make their nose run.

Many things can cause allergies that affect a person's breathing. They include dust mites, animal fur, and feathers. These allergies can also cause an **asthma** attack.

Worry

Worry or **stress** can cause some people to have an **asthma** attack. For example, if they hear their parents fighting, they may have an asthma attack.

Tests and other difficult things can also cause asthma. Asthma that is caused by the way a person feels happens more to older children and adults.

Narrower Airways

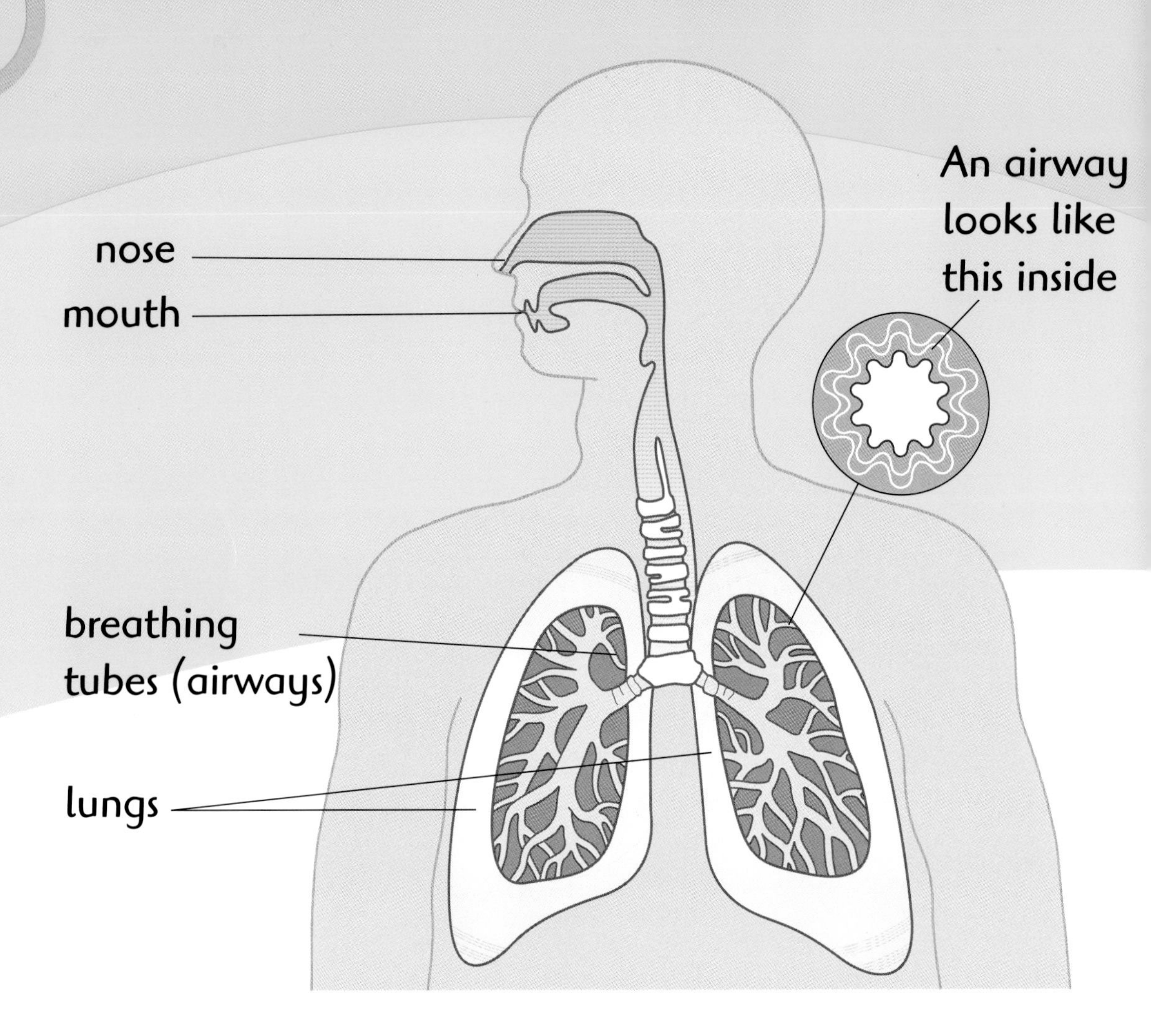

When you breathe in air, it passes through your nose or mouth into tubes that go to your **lungs. Asthma** affects these tiny **airways.**

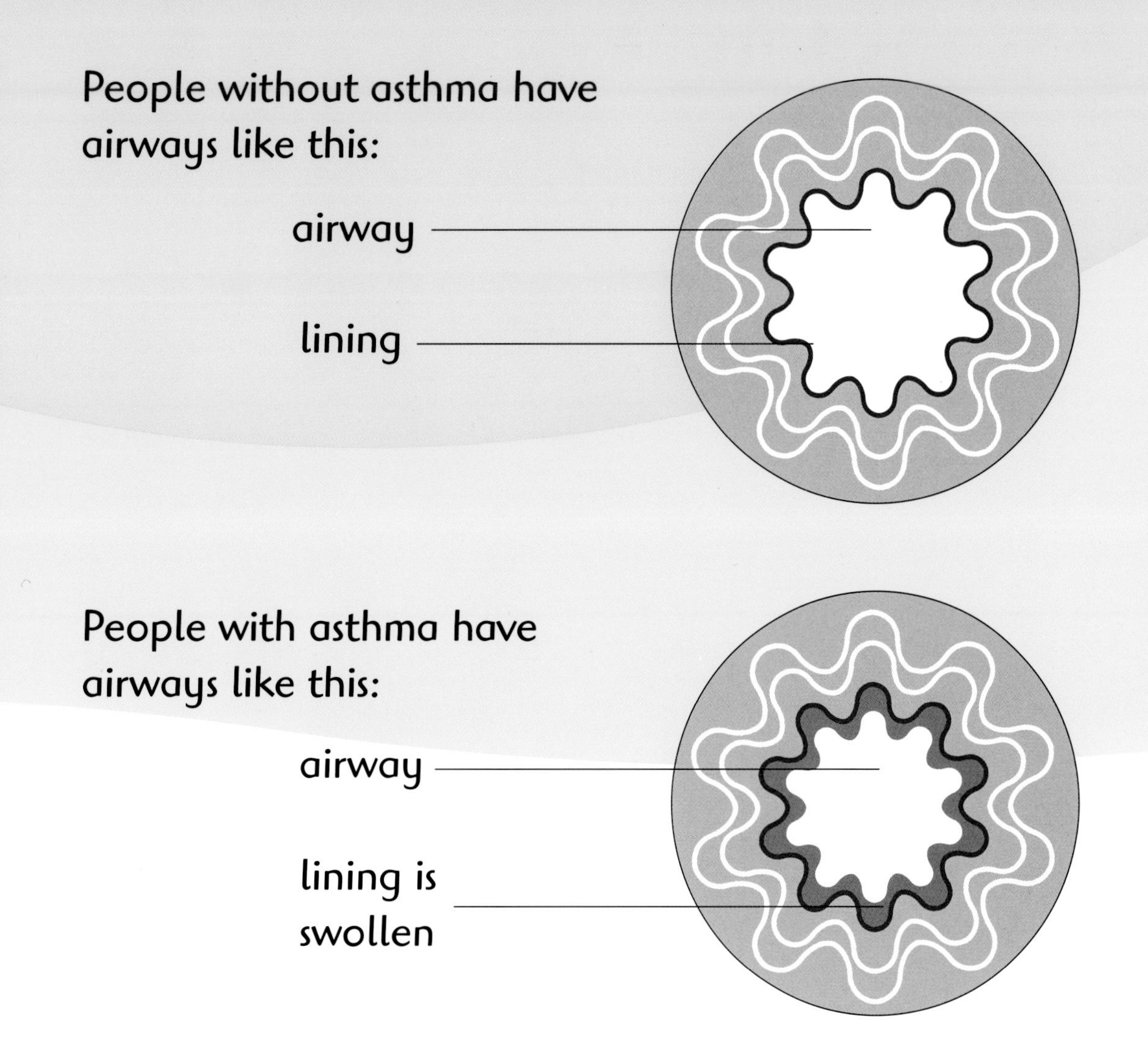

If you have asthma, the airways in your lungs are always a little **inflamed** and swollen. This makes them narrower than usual.

Tight Chest

This is what happens during an asthma attack:

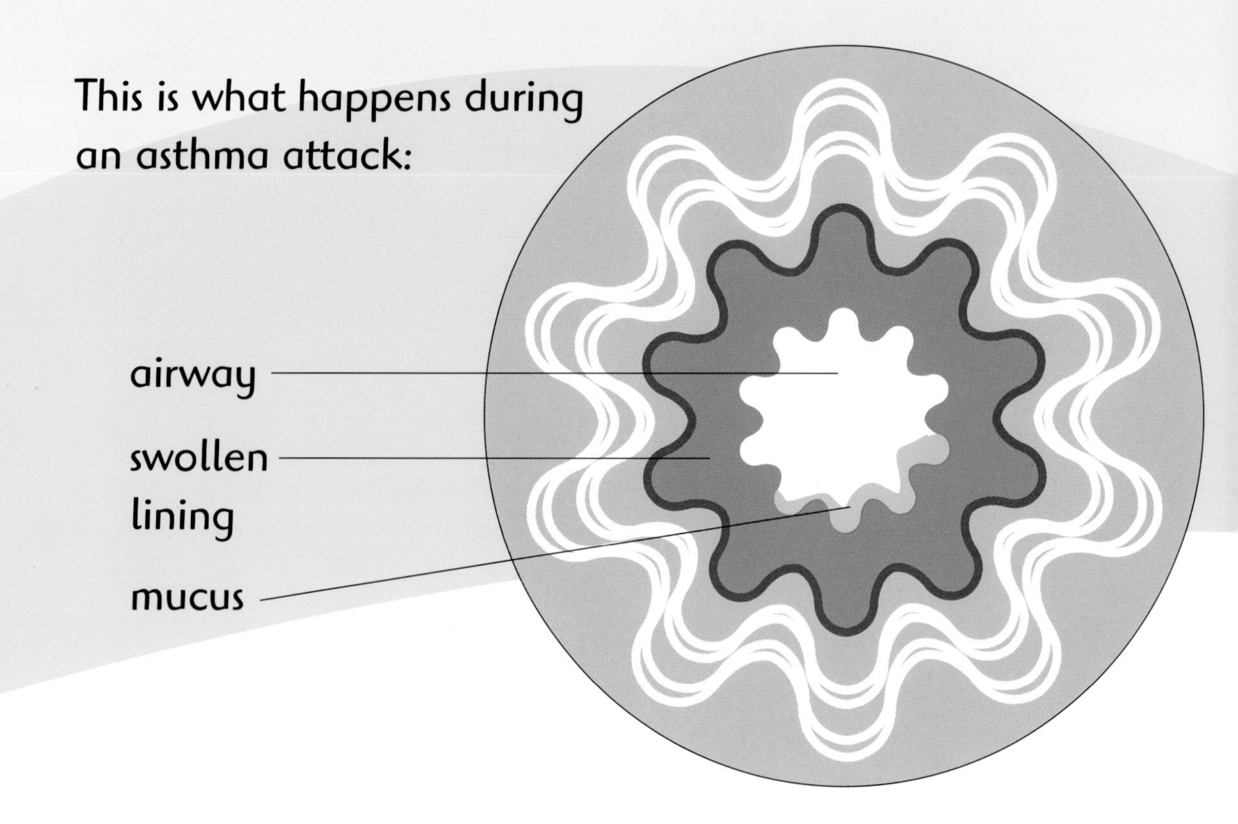

People sometimes know when they are about to have an **asthma** attack. Their chest feels tight. The **airways** in their **lungs** fill with thick, sticky **mucus.**

The mucus can almost block the airways completely. This makes it very difficult for the person to breathe in and out.

Coughing

During an **asthma** attack, the narrow tubes in the **lungs** become even narrower than usual. As the **airways** fill with **mucus,** the person usually begins to cough to try to get rid of it.

The person gasps for air, but cannot stop coughing. Eventually he or she may cough up some mucus and begin to feel better.

Testing for Asthma

If you think you may have **asthma,** an adult should take you to see a doctor. The doctor will use a **stethoscope** to listen to your **lungs** as you breathe in and out.

Doctors have a machine that tests for asthma. It shows how much air you can blow out in one puff. People with asthma blow out less air than other people.

Rescue Inhaler

People who have **asthma** attacks usually carry a **rescue inhaler.** It contains a medicine that widens the **airways** in the **lungs** and helps to loosen the **mucus.**

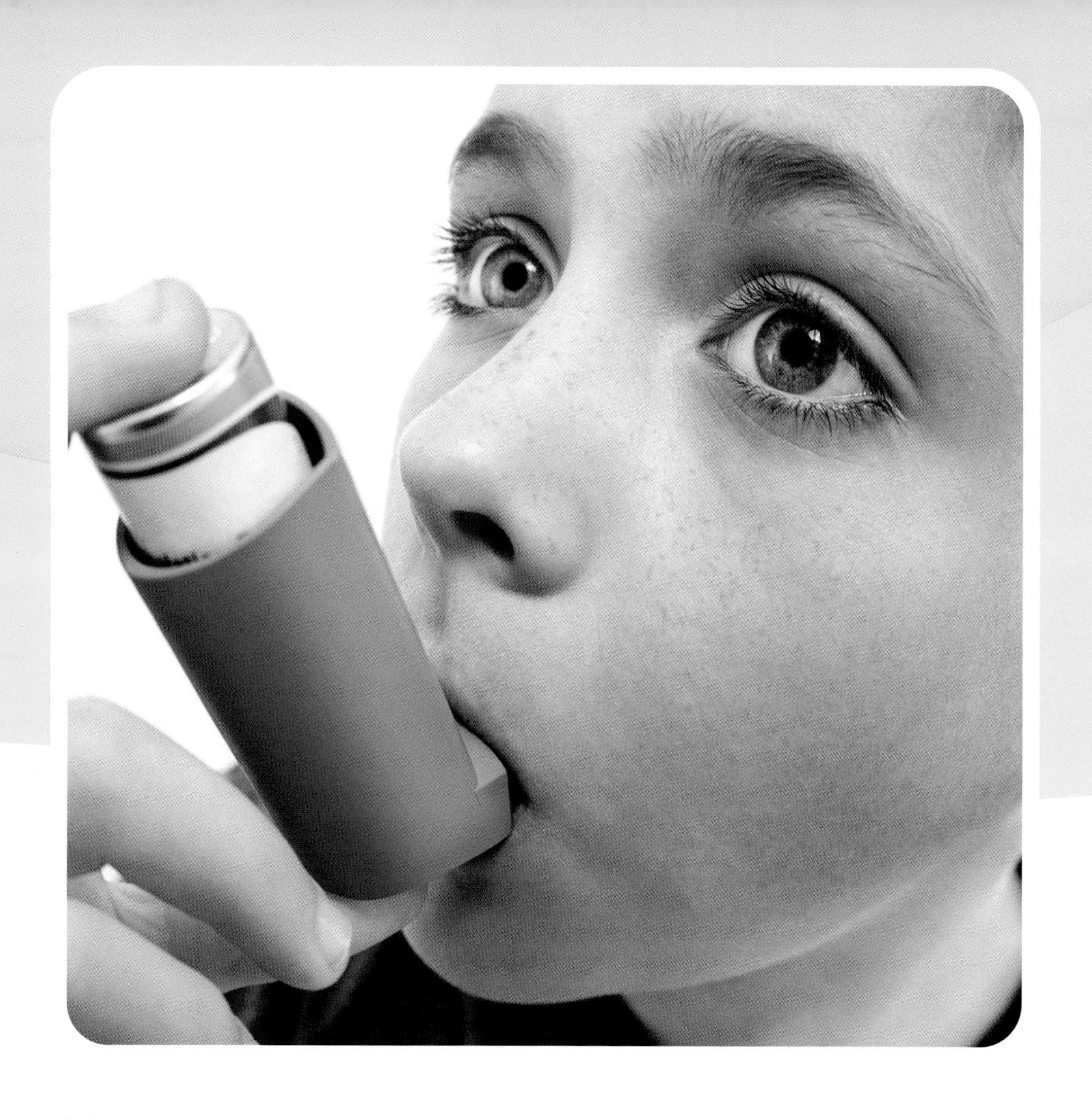

When people have asthma attacks, they breathe in slowly through their rescue inhaler. The medicine goes into their lungs. Soon they can breathe more easily.

Keep Calm

An **asthma** attack can be very scary for the person when it happens. It can also scare people nearby if they are not used to seeing an attack.

It is important that everyone keeps calm. Tell an adult that the person needs help. Help the person having the attack to relax. Give the person space to use a **rescue inhaler.**

Going to the Hospital

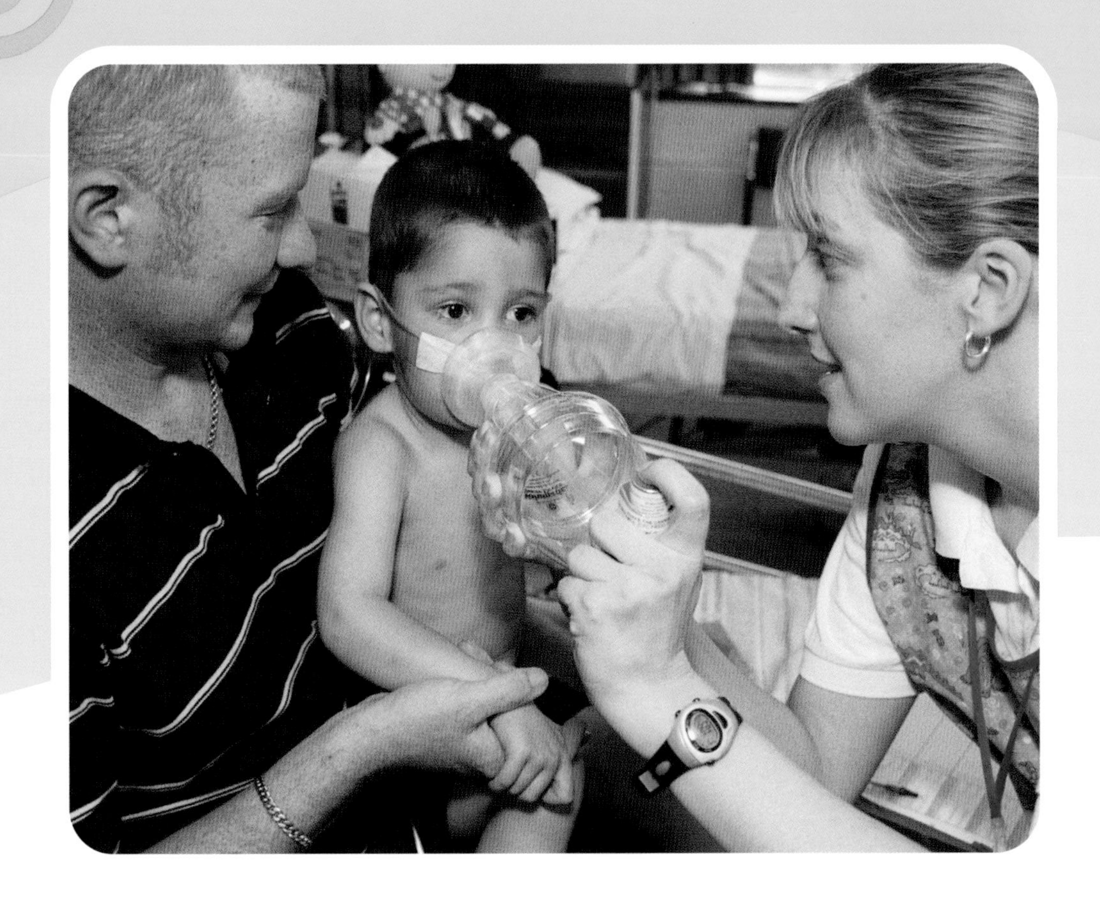

Most people can stop an **asthma** attack by using their **rescue inhaler.** But some people have to go to the hospital if an attack is very bad.

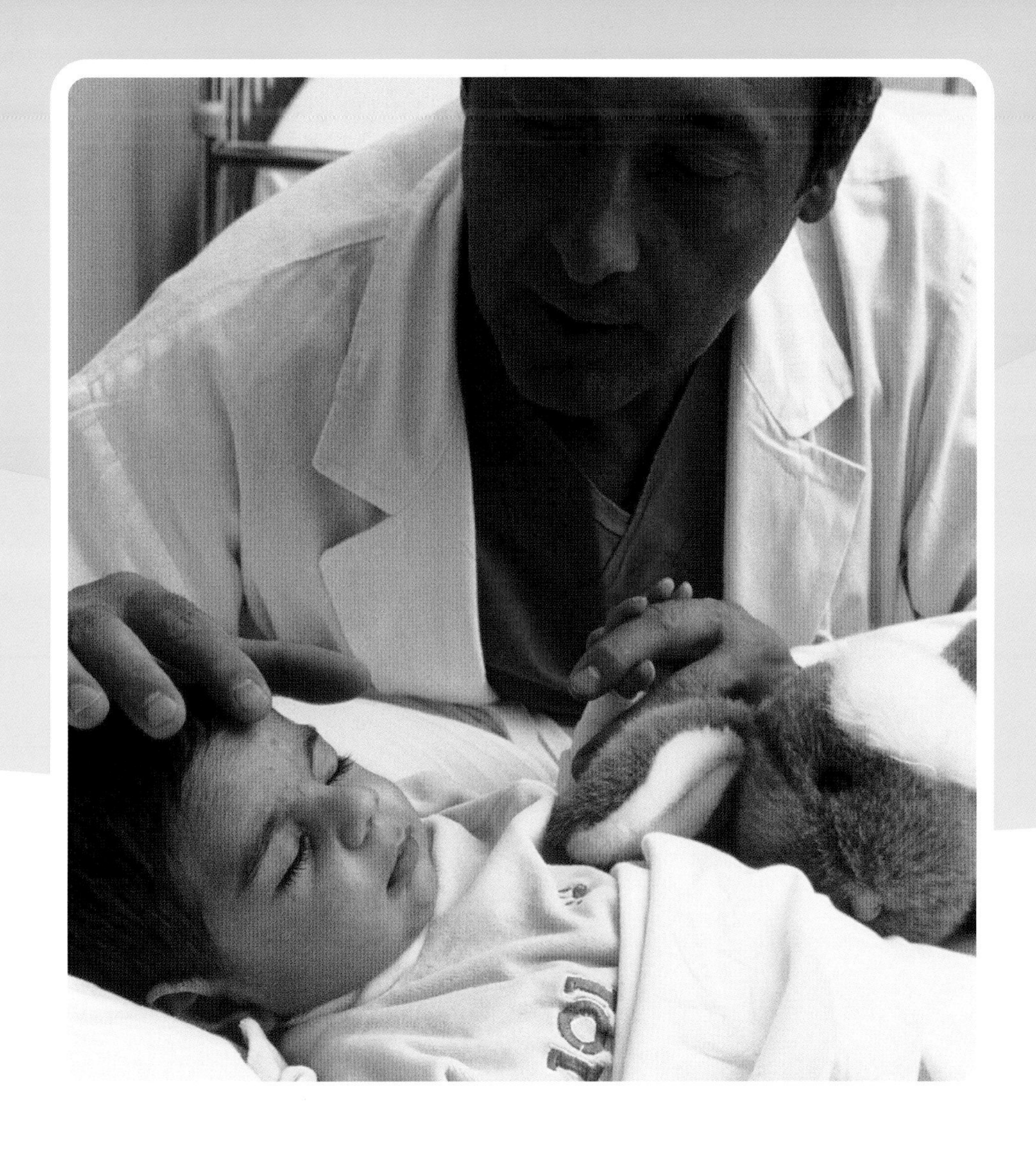

The hospital gives people medicine to help them breathe. They may have to stay in the hospital overnight until the doctor is sure that they are all right.

Preventing an Attack

A **controller inhaler** contains a medicine that makes the tubes in the **lungs** less swollen. This medicine can help to prevent an **asthma** attack.

Most people with asthma can live a normal life. They use the controller inhaler to stop an attack from happening. They should always carry the **rescue inhaler** in case they have an attack.

Glossary

airways narrow tubes in the lungs

allergic having an allergy

allergy condition when the body reacts to something that is safe to most people as if it were dangerous

asthma when the airways become narrow and full of mucus, making it hard to breathe in and out

controller inhaler device used for breathing in medicine

energetic using a lot of energy

inflamed red and swollen

irritate make part of the body itchy or sore

lungs parts of the body that air goes into when you breathe in

mucus slippery, sticky substance that is made inside the body and coats the air passages

pollen fine dust produced by flowering plants, grasses, some trees, and flowers

react respond to something

rescue inhaler device that contains a medicine for stopping asthma attacks

stethoscope device that doctors use to listen to your chest

stress feelings of worry and anxiety

More Books to Read

Royston, Angela. *Keep Healthy!*. Chicago: Heinemann Library, 2003.

Royston, Angela. *Why Do My Eyes Itch?: And Other Questions About Allergies.* Chicago: Heinemann Library, 2002.

Spilsbury, Louise. *What Does It Mean To Have Asthma?*. Chicago: Heinemann Library, 2001.

Index